SO-AXC-480

NORWEGIAN

Made Nice & Easy!™

Staff of Research & Education Association
Carl Fuchs, Language Program Director

Based on Language Courses developed by the
U.S. Government for Foreign Service Personnel

Research & Education Association
61 Ethel Road West
Piscataway, New Jersey 08854

Dr. M. Fogiel, Director

NORWEGIAN MADE NICE & EASY™

Copyright © 2001 by Research & Education Association. This copyright does not apply to the information included from U.S. Government publications, which was edited by Research & Education Association.

Printed in the United States of America

Library of Congress Control Number 00-193030

International Standard Book Number 0-87891-374-2

LANGUAGES MADE NICE & EASY is a trademark of Research & Education Association, Piscataway, New Jersey 08854

What This Guide Will Do For You

Whether travelling to a foreign country or to your favorite international restaurant, this *Nice & Easy* guide gives you just enough of the language to get around and be understood. Much of the material in this book was developed for government personnel who are often assigned to a foreign country on a moment's notice and need a quick introduction to the language.

In this handy and compact guide, you will find useful words and phrases, popular expressions, common greetings, and the words for numbers, money, and time. Every word or phrase is accompanied with the correct pronunciation and spelling. There is a vocabulary list for finding words quickly.

Generous margins on the pages allow you to make notes and remarks that you may find helpful.

If you expect to travel to Norway, the section on the country's history and relevant up-to-date facts will make your trip more informative and enjoyable. By keeping this guide with you, you'll be well prepared to understand as well as converse in Norwegian.

Carl Fuchs
Language Program Director

Contents

Norway

Facts & History

Official Name: Kingdom of Norway

Geography
Area (including the island territories of Svalbard and Jan Mayen): 385,364 sq. km. (150,000 sq. mi.); slightly larger than New Mexico.
Cities: *Capital* - Oslo (pop. 499,000). *Other cities* - Bergen (200,000), Trondheim (136,000), Stavanger (107,000).
Terrain: Rugged with high plateaus, steep fjords, mountains, and fertile valleys.
Climate: Temperate along the coast, colder inland.

People
Nationality: Noun and Norwegian(s).
Population: 4.4 million.
Annual growth rate: 0.5%.
Density: 13 per sq. km.

Ethnic groups: Norwegian (Nordic, Alpine, Baltic), Lapp (or Sami), a racial-cultural minority of 20,000; foreign nationals (225,000) from Nordic and other countries.
Religion: Evangelical Lutheran 94%.
Languages: Norwegian (official), Lapp.
Education: *Years compulsory* - 9. *Literacy* - 100%.
Health: *Life expectancy* - men 75 yrs; women 81 yrs.
Work force: Government, social, personal services - 39%. Wholesale and retail trade, hotels, restaurants - 17%. Manufacturing -15%. Transport and communications - 8%. Financing, insurance, real estate, business services - 8%. Agriculture, forestry, fishing - 5%. Construction - 6%. Oil extraction -1%.

Government
Type: Hereditary constitutional monarchy.
Independence: 1905.
Constitution: May 17, 1814.
Branches: *Executive* - king (chief of state), prime minister (head of government), Council of Ministers (cabinet). *Legislative* - modified unicameral parliament (Storting). *Judicial* - Supreme Court, appellate courts, city and county courts.
Political parties: Labor, Conservative, Center, Christian Democratic, Liberal, Socialist Left, Progress.
Administrative subdivisions: 18 fylker (counties), the city of Oslo, and Svalbard.
National holiday: May 17.

Flag: White cross with blue inner cross on red field. The white cross and red field are derived from the Danish flag; the blue cross was added to symbolize Norway's independence.

Economy
GDP (1997): $151 billion.
Annual growth rate (1997): 1.9%.
Per capita GDP (1997): $33,300.
Natural resources: Oil, gas, fish, timber, hydroelectric power, mineral ores.
Agriculture and fishing (2% of GDP): Arable land - 3%. Products - dairy, livestock, grain (barley, oats, wheat), potatoes and other vegetables, fruits and berries, furs, wool.
Industry: (manufacturing, 12% of GNP; oil, gas, shipping 16%; construction 4%) Types - food processing, pulp and paper, ships, aluminum, ferroalloys, iron and steel, nickel, zinc, nitrogen, fertilizers, transport equipment, hydroelectric power, refinery products, petrochemicals, electronics.

People and Culture
Ethnically, Norwegians are predominantly Germanic, although in the far north there are communities of Sami (Lapps) who came to the area more than 10,000 years ago, probably from central Asia. In recent years, Norway has become home to increasing numbers of immigrants, foreign workers, and asy-

lum-seekers from various parts of the world. Immigrants now total nearly 150,000; some have obtained Norwegian citizenship.

Although the Evangelical Lutheran Church is the state church, Norway has complete religious freedom. Education is free through the university level and is compulsory from ages 7 to 16. At least 12 months of military service and training are required of every eligible male. Norway's health system includes free hospital care, physician's compensation, and cash benefits during illness and pregnancy.

Norway is in the top rank of nations in the number of books printed per capita, even though Norwegian is one of the world's smallest language groups. Norway's most famous writer is the dramatist Henrik Ibsen. Artists Edvard Munch and Christian Krogh were Ibsen's contemporaries. Munch drew part of his inspiration from Europe and in turn exercised a strong influence on later European expressionists. Sculptor Gustav Vigeland has a permanent exhibition in the Vigeland Sculpture Park in Oslo. Musical development in Norway since Edvard Grieg has followed either native folk themes or, more recently, international trends.

History of Norway

The Viking period (9th to 11th centuries) was one of national unification and expansion. For their many expeditions the Vikings needed fast and seaworthy ships, and men with the skill to navigate them over open seas. The fact that these hardy men repeatedly voyaged to America and back is evidence enough of their mastery of the longships. The Sagas relate that it was Leif Eriksson who discovered "Wineland the Good" in the year 1001, but present day scholars claim that other Vikings had reached America before him. The Viking Age finally culminated in 1066 when the Norwegian King Harald Hardruler and his men were defeated at the Battle of Stamford Bridge in England.

The late Middle Ages were a period of marked economic deterioration in Norway. The population had been drastically reduced by the ravages of the Black Death and other plagues during the fourteenth century. Many farms in the marginal areas were deserted, and incomes sank. Some claim that a worsening of the climate and the grip of the Hanseatic League on Norwegian economy were the cause of the decline. Others believe that a steady impoverishment of the soil contributed to the deterioration.

The economic depression brought political consequences in its wake. Denmark assumed increasing importance as the major Nordic land. Danish and German nobles were appointed to the highest official offices. Lands and episcopal residences passed into foreign hands. The Norwegian nobility dwindled. Thus was the will and the ability for national self-assertion gradually sapped.

The Norwegian royal line died out in 1387, and the country entered a period of union with Denmark. By 1586, Norway had become part of the Danish Kingdom. In 1814, as a result of the Napoleonic wars, Norway was separated from Denmark and combined with Sweden. The union persisted until 1905, when Sweden recognized Norwegian independence.

The Norwegian Government offered the throne of Norway to Danish Prince Carl in 1905. After a plebiscite approving the establishment of a monarchy, the parliament unanimously elected him king. He took the name of Haakon VII, after the kings of independent Norway. Haakon died in 1957 and was succeeded by his son, Olav V, who died in January 1991. Upon Olav's death, his son Harald was crowned as King Harald V. Norway was a nonbelligerent during World War I, but as a result of the German invasion and occupation during World War II, Norwegians generally became skeptical of the concept of neutrality and turned instead to collective security. Norway was one of the signers of the North Atlantic Treaty in 1949 and was a founding member of the United Nations. The first UN General Secretary, Trygve Lie, was a Norwegian. Under the terms of the will of Alfred Nobel, the Storting (Parliament) elects the five members of the Norwegian Nobel Committee who award the Nobel Peace Prize to champions of peace.

Government

The functions of the King are mainly ceremonial, but he has influence as the symbol of national unity. Although the 1814 constitution grants important executive powers to the king, these are almost always exercised by the Council of Ministers in the name of the King (King's Council). The Council of Ministers consists of a prime minister — chosen by the political parties represented in the Storting — and other ministers. The 165 members of the Storting are elected from 18 fylker (counties) for 4-year terms according to a complicated system of proportional representation. The special High Court of the Realm hears impeachment cases; the regular courts include the Supreme Court (17 permanent judges and a president), courts of appeal, city and county courts, the labor court, and conciliation councils. Judges attached to regular courts are appointed by the King in council after nomination by the Ministry of Justice.

Economy

Norway is one of the world's richest countries. It has an important stake in promoting a liberal environment for foreign trade. Its large shipping fleet is one of the most modern among maritime nations. Metals, pulp and paper products, chemicals, shipbuilding, and fishing are the most significant traditional industries.

Norway's emergence as a major oil and gas producer in the mid-1970s transformed the economy. Large sums of investment capital poured into the offshore oil sector, leading to greater increases in Norwegian production costs and wages than in the rest of Western Europe up to the time of the global recovery of the mid-1980s. The influx of oil revenue also permitted Norway to expand an already extensive social welfare system. Norway's exports have continued to grow, largely because of favorable world demand for oil and gas. Moreover, the flight of Norwegian-owned ships from the country's traditional register ended in 1987, as the government established an international register, replete with tax breaks and relief from national crewmember requirements.

Early morning Bergen

2

Royal Palace Slottet, Oslo

Northern coast at night

4

Eiksdal, Møre og Romsdal

The Aurlandsfjord

Hints on Pronunciation

All the words and phrases are written in a spelling which you read like English. Each letter or combination of letters is used for the sound it normally represents in English and it *always* stands for the same sound. Thus, *oo* is always to be read as in *too, boot, tooth, roost.* Say these words and then pronounce the vowel sound by itself. That is the sound you must use every time you see *oo* in the Pronunciation column. If you should use some other sound—for example, the one in *blood* or the one in *door*—you might be misunderstood.

Kristiansund

Syllables that are accented—that is, pronounced louder than others—are written in capital letters. Curved lines (‿) are used to show sounds that are pronounced together without any break; for example, K‿NAHP-per meaning "buttons."

Special Points

AY
as in *day*, *say*, *may*. Example: *NAY* meaning "no."

AY
when underlined, stands for a sound a little different from the one in *day*, *say*, *may*, *play*. Listen for it on the phonograph record. Example: *TRAY* meaning "three."

E *or* EH
as in *let*, *bell*, *bet*. Example: *FEM* meaning "five"; *ho-TEL-eh* meaning "the hotel."

EE
when underlined, stands for a sound we don't have in English. To make it, round your lips as though to say *oo* and without moving them say *ee*. Example: *TEE-veh* meaning "twenty."

ER
when underlined stands for a sound something like the *er* in *her*. Example: *BRER* meaning "bread."

The Geirangerfjord

Bud

Ă	with a curved line over it stands for the sound we have in *hat*, *bat*, *mat*. Example: *HĂR* meaning "Mr."
A *or* **AH**	as in *ah*, *pa*, *father*, *calm*. Examples: *YA* meaning "yes," *TAHK* meaning "Thank you."

USEFUL WORDS AND PHRASES

GREETINGS AND GENERAL PHRASES

English	Pronunciation	Norwegian Spelling
Hello	ha-LO	Hallo
Good day	go DA	God dag
Good morning	go MAWRN	God morgen
Good evening	go AHF-TEN	God aften
or in the country	go KˇVEL	God kveld
Mr. Olsen	hår OAL-sen	Herr Olsen

Notice the sound written *ă* with a curved line over it in the last word. Listen again and repeat: HĂR, HĂR. It is the same sound we have in *bat, hat,* etc. Try just the sound again: *ă, ă.*

Mrs. Olsen	froo OAL-sen	Fru Olsen
Miss Olsen	FRER-ken OAL-sen	Frøken Olsen
How are you?	VOR-dahn HAR dee deh?	Hvordan har De det?
Fine, thank you	tahk, BRA	Takk, bra

ă *as in* bat; e *or* eh *as in* bet

Fishing cabins in northern coast

Hardangerfjord

The Norwegian expression for "please" really means "Be so kind as to ____." It is:

	VÅR saw SNIL aw ____	Vær så snild å ____
Please help me	VÅR saw SNIL aw YELP-eh MAY	Vær så snild å hjelpe meg
Thank you	TAHK	Takk
Excuse me	OON-shil	Unnskyld
Yes	YA	Ja
No	NAY	Nei
Do you understand?	fawr-STAWR dee?	Forstår De?

13

English	Pronunciation	Norwegian Spelling
I don't under- stand	YAY fawr- STAWR IK-keh	Jeg forstår ikke
Speak slowly	SNAHK lahng- SAWMT	Snakk langsomt

You have probably noticed that Norwegian has a definite sing-song quality. This is very important in the language, and you should imitate each phrase exactly as you hear it.

Please repeat	VÅR saw SNIL aw YEN-TA	Vær så snild å gjenta

Stavanger

LOCATION

When you need directions to get somewhere, use the phrase "Where is" and then add the words you need.

Where is ___?	vor ÅR ___?	Hvor er ___?
the restaurant	ka-FAY-en	kaféen
Where is the restaurant?	VOR är ka-FAY-en?	Hvor er kaféen?
the hotel	ho-TEL-eh	hotellet
Where is the hotel?	VOR är ho-TEL-eh?	Hvor er hotellet?
the streetcar	TRIK-ken	trikken
Where is the streetcar?	VOR är TRIK-ken?	Hvor er trikken?
the railroad station	sta-SHO-nen	stasjonen
Where is the railroad station?	VOR är sta-SHO-nen?	Hvor er stasjonen?
the toilet	twa-LET-teh	toalettet
Where is the toilet?	VOR är twa-LET-teh?	Hvor er toalettet?

ä *as in* bat; e *or* eh *as in* bet

DIRECTIONS

The answer to your question "Where is such and such?" may be "To the right" or "To the left" or "Straight ahead," so you need to know these phrases.

To the right	til HAY-reh	Til høyre
To the left	til VEN-streh	Til venstre
Straight ahead	ret FRAHM	Rett fram

It is sometimes useful to say "Show me the way."

Will you show me the way?	KAHN dee VEE-seh may VAY-en?	Kan De vise meg vegen?

If you are driving and ask the distance to another town it will be given to you in kilometers, not miles.

Kilometer	chee-lo-MET-er	kilometer

One kilometer equals ⅝ of a mile.

Søragadå in Skudeneshavn

NUMBERS

You need to know the numbers.

One	AYN	en
Two	TO	to
Three	TRAY	tre
Four	FEE-REH	fire
Five	FEM	fem
Six	SEKS	seks
Seven	SHOO	sju
Eight	AWT-TEH	åtte
Nine	NEE	ni
Ten	TEE	ti
Eleven	EL-VEH	elleve
Twelve	TAWL	tolv
Thirteen	TRET-TEN	tretten
Fourteen	F_YOR-TEN	fjorten
Fifteen	FEM-TEN	femten
Sixteen	SAYSS-TEN	seksten
Seventeen	SUT-TEN	sytten

ă *as in* bat; e *or* eh *as in* bet

Geirangerfjord

English	Pronunciation	Norwegian Spelling
Eighteen	AHT-TEN	atten
Nineteen	NIT-TEN	nitten
Twenty	T<u>EE</u>-VEH	tyve

In the last word you heard a sound you must practice. It is written in your Guide as double *ee* with a line underneath. Listen again and repeat: *T<u>EE</u>-VEH*, *T<u>EE</u>-VEH*. Round your lips as though to say *oo* and without moving them say *ee*. Try just the sound again: <u>*ee*</u>, <u>*ee*</u>.

For "twenty-one," "twenty-two," etc., you say "one and twenty," "two and twenty," etc.

English	Pronunciation	Norwegian Spelling
Twenty-one	<u>AY</u>N o T<u>EE</u>-VEH	en og tyve
Twenty-two	TO o T<u>EE</u>-VEH	to og tyve
Thirty	TRED-VEH	tredve
Forty	FUR-tee	førti
Fifty	FEM-tee	femti
Sixty	SEKS-tee	seksti
Seventy	SUT-tee	sytti
Eighty	AWT-tee	åtti

å as in bất; e or eh as in bet

English	Pronunciation	Norwegian Spelling
Ninety	NIT-tee	nitti
One hundred	HOON-DREH	hundre
One thousand	TOO-sen	tusen

WHAT'S THIS?

When you want to know the name of something you can say "What's this?" and point to the thing you mean.

What is ___?	va ĂR ___?	Hvad er ___?
this	DET-TEH	dette
What's this?	VA är DET-TEH?	Hvad er dette?

Bryggen, (The Wharf), Bergen

ASKING FOR THINGS

When you want something, use the phrase "Have you?" or "Please give me" and then add the words you need.

Have you ___?	HAR dee ___?	Har De ___?
cigarettes	sig-ah-RET-TER	sigaretter
Have you cigarettes?	HAR dee sig-ah-RET-TER?	Har De sigaretter?
Please give me ___	VÅR saw SNIL aw YEE may ___	Vær så snild å gi meg ___
food	MAHT	mat
Please give me food	VÅR saw SNIL aw YEE may MAHT	Vær så snild å gi meg mat

Here are the words for some of the things you may require.

bread	BR<u>ER</u>	brød

In the last word you heard another sound you must practice. It is written in your Guide as *er*.

Listen again and repeat: *BR<u>ER</u>, BR<u>ER</u>.* It sounds something like the *er* sound in *her* said without the *r*. Try just the sound again: *<u>er</u>, <u>er</u>.*

English	Pronunciation	Norwegian Spelling
butter	SM<u>E</u>RR	smør
soup	SOOP-PEH	suppe
fish	FISK	fisk
meat	CHUT	kjøtt

Notice the sound written *ch* in the last word. Listen again and repeat: *CHUT, CHUT.* You will be understood if you use the *ch* sound in *church;* but try to imitate the Norwegian sound. Try just the sound again: *ch, ch.*

chicken	CHIL-LING	kylling
lamb	FAW-reh-CHUT	fårekjøtt
veal	KAHL-veh-CHUT	kalvekjøtt
beef	BIF	biff
pork	FLESK	flesk
eggs	EG	egg
vegetables	GRUN-SA-ker	grønnsaker
potatoes	po-T<u>A</u>Y-ter	poteter
beans	BUN-NER	bønner
fruit	FROOKT	frukt
apples	EP-LER	epler

à *as in* bat; e *or* eh *as in* bet

English	Pronunciation	Norwegian Spelling
salad	sa-LAHT	salat
sugar	SOOK-ker	sukker
salt	SAHLT	salt
pepper	PEP-PER	pepper
water	VAHN	vann
milk	MELK	melk
tea	TAY	te
a cup of coffee	ayn kawp KA-fay	en kopp kaffe
a glass of beer	et glahss ULL	et glass øll
a bottle of wine	ayn FLA-skeh VEEN	en flaske vin
matches	FEER-shtik-ker	fyrstikker

Puffin, Norwegian coastline

MONEY

To find out how much things cost, you say:

how much	vor MA̱Y-GET	hvor meget
costs	KAW-STER	koster
this	DET-TEH	dette
How much does this cost?	vor MA̱Y-get KAW-ster DET-TEH?	Hvor meget koster dette?

TIME

To find out what time it is, you say really, "What is the clock?"

| What time is it? | va år KLAWK-KEN? | Hvad er klokken? |

Viking ship

ă *as in* bat; e *or* eh *as in* bet

For "It's one o'clock," "It's two o'clock," etc., you say "The clock is one," "The clock is two," etc.

It's one o'clock	KLAWK-ken är ET	Klokken er ett
It's two o'clock	KLAWK-ken är TO	Klokken er to

If someone asks you what time it is, you can answer with the number alone.

One o'clock	ET	ett
Two o'clock	TO	to

Half past four is "half five."

Half past four	HAHL FEM	halv fem

To find out when a movie starts or when a train or bus leaves, you say:

when	NAWR	når
starts	B'YIN-ner	begynner
the movie	CHEE-noan	kinoen
When does the **movie start?**	NAWR B'YIN- ner CHEE- noan?	Når begynner kinoen?

Street in Lillehammer

English	Pronunciation	Norwegian Spelling
leaves	GAWR	går
the train	TAWG-eh	toget
When does the train leave?	NAWR gawr TAWG-eh?	Når går toget?

English	Pronunciation	Norwegian Spelling
bus	BOOSS-en	bussen
When does the bus leave?	NAWR gawr BOOSS-en?	Når går bussen?
Yesterday	ee-GAWR	igår
Today	ee-DA	idag
Tomorrow	ee-MAWRN	imorgen

The days of the week are:

Sunday	SUN-da	søndag
Monday	MAHN-da	mandag
Tuesday	TEERSH-da	tirsdag
Wednesday	OANSS-da	onsdag
Thursday	TAWRSH-da	torsdag
Friday	FR<u>AY</u>-da	fredag
Saturday	LUR-da	lørdag

OTHER USEFUL PHRASES

The following phrases will be useful.

What is your name?	va H<u>AY</u>-TER DEE?	Hvad heter De?

ä *as in* bat; e *or* eh *as in* bet

Skudeneshavn

English	Pronunciation	Norwegian Spelling
My name is ___	yay HAY-TER ___	Jeg heter ___
How do you say "table" (or anything else) in Norwegian?	va HAY-TER "table" paw NAWRSHK?	Hvad heter "table" på norsk?
I am an American	YAY är ah-may-ree-KA-ner	Jeg er amerikaner
I am a friend	YAY är ayn VEN	Jeg er en venn
Where is the nearest town?	VOR är den NÄR-mest-eh BEE?	Hvor er den nær-meste by?
Please go with me	VÄR saw SNIL aw GAW meh MAY	Vær så snild å gå med meg

NOTE: The Norwegian word for "good-by" is *ahd-YER* (adjø).

28

ADDITIONAL EXPRESSIONS

Come in!	KAWM in!	Kom inn!
Have a seat!	TA plahss!	Ta plass!
Glad to know you	HIG-gel-ee aw S<u>A</u>Y dem	Hyggelig å se Dem
I don't know	yay VAYT ik-keh	Jeg vet ikke
I think so	yay TROR deh	Jeg tror det
I don't think so	yay TROR IK-keh DEH	Jeg tror ikke det
Maybe	KAHN-sheh	Kanskje
Stop!	STAHN-seh! *or* STAWP!	Stanse! Stopp!
Come here!	KAWM HEET!	Kom hit!
Quickly!	STRAHKS!	Straks!
Come quickly!	KAWM STRAHKS!	Kom straks!
Go quickly!	GAW STRAHKS!	Gå straks!
I am hungry	YAY år SOOL-ten	Jeg er sulten
I am thirsty	YAY år TURSHT	Jeg er tørst
I am tired	YAY år TRET	Jeg er trett

å as in bat; e or eh as in bet

Floro

English	Pronunciation	Norwegian Spelling
I am lost	YAY har GAWT may BORT	Jeg har gått meg bort
Help!	YELP!	Hjelp!
Bring help!	skahf YELP!	Skaff hjelp!
I'll pay you	yay VIL B'TA- leh dem	Jeg vil betale Dem
Which way is north?	VOR åł NOR?	Hvor er nord?
south	S<u>EE</u>D	syd
east	UST	øst
west	VEST	vest

English	Pronunciation	Norwegian Spelling
Which is the road to Oslo?	VOR gawr VAY-en til O-slo?	Hvor går vegen til Oslo?
Draw me a map	TAYN et KART fawr MAY	Tegn et kart for meg
Take me to a doctor	SEN may til ayn DAWK-tor	Send meg til en doktor
Take me to the hospital	SEN may til ho-spee-TA-leh	Send meg til hospitalet
How far is it?	vor LAHNKT år DEH?	Hvor langt er det?
Is it far?	år deh LAHNKT?	Er det langt?
Is it nearby?	år deh ee når-HAY-ten?	Er det i·nær-heten?
Danger!	FA-reh!	Fare!
Gas!	GAHSS!	Gass!
Take cover!	SERK DEK-ning!	Søk dekning!
Watch out!	PAHSS paw!	Pass på!
Wait a minute!	VENT lit!	Vent litt!
Good luck!	LIK-keh TIL!	Lykke til!

å *as in* bat; e *or* eh *as in* bet

FILL-IN SENTENCES

In this section you will find a number of sentences, each containing a blank space which can be filled in with any one of the words in the list that follows. For example, if you want to say "Where is the post office?" find the fill-in sentence for "Where is ___?" and, in the list following the sentence, the word for "the post office." You then combine them as follows:

Where is ___?	VOR är ___?	Hvor er ___?
the post office	PAWST-koan-to-reh	postkontoret
Where is the post office?	VOR är PAWST-koan-to-reh?	Hvor er postkon-toret?

Flydalsjuvet Gorge, Geiranger

English	Pronunciation	Norwegian Spelling
Have you ___?	HAR dee ___?	Har De ___?

NOTE: When you want to buy something or ask someone for something in Norwegian, you don't as a rule say "I want" or "I would like." Instead you say "Have you" and then add the name of the thing you want.

English	Pronunciation	Norwegian Spelling
Let me have ___	LA may FAW ___	La meg få ___
Give me ___	YEE may ___	Gi meg ___
Where can I get ___?	VOR kahn yay FAW ___?	Hvor kan jeg få ___?
Where can I buy ___?	VOR kahn yay faw CHER-peh ___?	Hvor kan jeg få kjøpe ___?
I have ___	YAY har ___	Jeg har ___
We have ___	VEE har ___	Vi har ___
I don't have ___	YAY har IK-keh ___	Jeg har ikke ___
We don't have ___	VEE har IK-keh ___	Vi har ikke ___

EXAMPLE

English	Pronunciation	Norwegian Spelling
Have you ___?	HAR dee ___?	Har De ___?
drinking water	DRIK-keh-VAHN	drikkevann

ă *as in* bat; e *or* eh *as in* bet   **33**

English	Pronunciation	Norwegian Spelling
Have you drinking water?	HAR dee DRIK-keh-VAHN?	Har De drikke-vann?
boiled water	KOAKT VAHN	kokt vann
cabbage	KAWL	kål
carrots	GOO-leh-rut-ter	gulerøtter
cheese	OAST	ost
chocolate	sho-ko-LA-deh	sjokolade
grapes	DROO-er	druer
ham	SHIN-keh	skinke
onions	L<u>E</u>RK	løk
pears	PĂR-er	pærer
peas	ĂR-ter	erter
a cup	<u>ay</u>n KAWP	en kopp
a fork	<u>ay</u>n GAHF-fel	en gaffel
a glass	et GLAHSS	et glass
a knife	<u>ay</u>n K‿NEEV	en kniv

34

English	Pronunciation	Norwegian Spelling
a plate	a̲yn tahl-LÅR-ken	en tallerken
a spoon	a̲yn SH<u>AY</u>	en skje
a bed	a̲yn SENG	en seng
blankets	ool-TEP-per	ulltepper
a mattress	a̲yn ma-DRAHSS	en madrass
a pillow	a̲yn POO-teh	en pute
a room	et ROOM	et rom
sheets	LA-ken-er	lakener
a towel	et HAWN-kleh	et håndkle
cigars	see-GA-rer	sigarer
a pipe	a̲yn PEE-peh	en pipe
tobacco	to-BAHK	tobakk
ink	BLEK	blekk
paper	pa-PEER	papir
a pen	a̲yn PEN	en penn
a pencil	a̲yn bl<u>ee</u>-AHNT	en blyant

English	Pronunciation	Norwegian Spelling
a comb	a̲yn KAHM	en kam
hot water	VARMT VAHN	varmt vann
a razor	a̲yn bar-BA̲YR-he̲r-vel	en barberhøvel
razor blades	bar-BA̲YR-blahd	barberblad
a shaving brush	a̲yn bar-BA̲YR-koast	en barberkost
shaving soap	bar-BA̲YR-saw-peh	barbersåpe
soap	SAW-peh	såpe
a tooth-brush	a̲yn TAHN-bursh-teh	en tannbørste
tooth paste	TAHN-kra̲ym or TAHN-pa-sta	tannkrem tannpasta
a handker-chief	et TURK-leh	et tørkle
a raincoat	a̲yn RAYN-frahk	en regnfrakk
a shirt	a̲yn SHOR-teh	en skjorte
shoe laces	sko-LISS-ser	skolisser
shoe polish	sko-SVĂR-teh	skosverte

ă *as in* bat; e *or* eh *as in* bet

Lofoten Islands

37

English	Pronunciation	Norwegian Spelling
shoes	SKO	sko
underwear	oon-er-TAY	undertøy
buttons	K‿NAHP-per	knapper
a needle or a pin	ayn NAWL	en nål
safety pins	sik-ker-hayts-NAW-ler	sikkerhetsnåler
thread	TRAW	tråd
adhesive tape	PLA-ster	plaster
an antiseptic	et ahn-tee-SEP-tisk-MID-del	et antiseptisk-middel
aspirin	ah-spee-REEN	aspirin
a bandage	ayn bahn-DA-sheh	en bandasje
cotton	BO-mool	bomull
a disinfectant	et dess-in-fee-SAY-ren-deh-MID-del	et desinfiserende-middel
iodine	YAWD	jodd

å *as in* bat; e *or* eh *as in* bet

English	Pronunciation	Norwegian Spelling
a laxative	et AHV-f<u>er</u>-ringss-MID-del	et avføringsmiddel
gasoline	ben-SEEN	bensin

English	Pronunciation	Norwegian Spelling
I want to ___	yay VIL ___	Jeg vil ___
May I ___?	kahn yay FAW ___?	Kan jeg få ___?

EXAMPLE

English	Pronunciation	Norwegian Spelling
I want to ___	yay VIL ___	Jeg vil ___
eat	SPEE-seh	spise
I want to eat	yay VIL SPEE-seh	Jeg vil spise

English	Pronunciation	Norwegian Spelling
buy it	CH<u>ER</u>-peh deh	kjøpe det
pay	B'TA-leh	betale
rest	VEE-leh	hvile
sleep	SAW-veh	sove
take a bath	TA et BAHD	ta et bad
wash up	VA-skeh may	vaske meg

ä *as in* b**a**t; e *or* eh *as in* b**e**t

In a barber shop you say *bar-BAY-ress* (barberes) if you want a shave and *KLIP-pess* (klippes) if you want a haircut.

Where is there ___?	VOR år deh ___?	Hvor er det ___?

EXAMPLE

Where is there ___?	VOR år deh ___?	Hvor er det ___?
a garage	ayn ga-RA-sheh	en garasje
Where is there a garage?	VOR år deh ayn ga-RA-sheh?	Hvor er det en garasje?

a clothing store	ayn KLAY-fawr-ret-ning	en kleforretning
a drugstore *or* pharmacy	et ah-po-TAYK	et apotek
a filling station	ayn ben-SEEN-sta-shoan	en bensinstasjon
a grocery	ayn ko-lo-nee-AHL-hahnd-el	en kolonialhandel
a house	et HOOSS	et hus
a laundry	et va-skay-REE	et vaskeri

ă *as in* bat; e *or* eh *as in* bet

English	Pronunciation	Norwegian Spelling
a mechanic	ayn may-KA-nee-ker	en mekaniker
a porter	ayn BĂR-er	en bærer
a servant	ayn T‿YAY-ner	en tjener
a spring	ayn CHIL-deh	en kilde
a well	ayn BRUN	en brønn

Where is ___?	VOR år ___?	Hvor er ___?
How far is ___?	vor LAHNKT år deh til ___?	Hvor langt er det til ___?

EXAMPLE

Where is ___?	VOR år ___?	Hvor er ___?
the barber	bar-BAY-ren	barberen
Where is the barber?	VOR år bar-BAY-ren?	Hvor er barberen?

the dentist	TAHN-lay-gen	tannlægen
the doctor	DAWK-to-ren	doktoren
the policeman	po-lee-TEE-eh	politiet

ă *as in* băt; e *or* eh *as in* bĕt   **41**

English	Pronunciation	Norwegian Spelling
the shoe-maker	sko-MA-ker-en	skomakeren
the tailor	SKRED-der-en	skredderen
the bridge	BROAN	broen
the bus	BOOSS-en	bussen
the camp	LAY-ren	leiren
the church	CHEER-ken	kirken
the city or the large town	B<u>EE</u>-en	byen
the high-way	HO-ved-VAY-en	hovedvegen
the hospital	ho-spee-TA-leh	hospitalet
the main street	HO-ved-GA-ten	hovedgaten
the market	TAWR-veh	torvet
the police station	po-lee-TEE-sta-sho-nen	politistasjonen
the post office	PAWST-koan-to-reh	postkontoret
the rail-road	yărn-BA-nen	jernbanen

ă *as in* băt; e *or* eh *as in* bĕt

English	Pronunciation	Norwegian Spelling
the river	ELV-ah	elva
the road	VAY-en	vegen
the small town	LAHNTS-b<u>ee</u>-en	landsbyen
the street-car	TRIK-ken	trikken
the tele-graph office	tel-eg-RAHF-koan-to-reh	telegrafkontoret
the tele-phone	tel-eh-FO-nen	telefonen

I am ___	YAY år ___	Jeg er ___
He is ___	HAHN år ___	Han er ___
Who is ___?	VEM år ___?	Hvem er ___?
Are you ___?	ÅR dee ___?	Er De ___?

EXAMPLE

I am ___	YAY år ___	Jeg er ___
hungry	SOOL-ten	sulten
I am hungry	YAY år SOOL-ten	Jeg er sulten

ä *as in* bat; e *or* eh *as in* bet   **43**

Hjølmoberget, Eidsfjord

English	Pronunciation	Norwegian Spelling
sick	S<u>EE</u>K	syk
thirsty	TURSHT	tørst
tired	TRET	trett
wounded	SAW-ret	såret

We are ___	VEE ăr ___	Vi er ___
They are ___	DEE ăr ___	De er ___

EXAMPLE

We are ___	VEE ăr ___	Vi er ___
hungry	SOOLT-neh	sultne
We are hungry	VEE ăr SOOLT-neh	Vi er sultne

sick	S<u>EE</u>-keh	syke
thirsty	TURSH-teh	tørste
tired	TRET-teh	trette
wounded	SAW-ret	såret

ă *as in* bat; e *or* eh *as in* bet

Mount Fløyen, Bergen

English	Pronunciation	Norwegian Spelling
Is it ___?	ÅR deh ___?	Er det ___?
It is ___	DEH år ___	Det er ___
It is not ___	DEH år IK-keh ___	Det er ikke ___
It is too ___	DEH år fawr ___	Det er for ___
It is very ___	DEH år MAY-get ___	Det er meget ___
This is ___	DET-teh år ___	Dette er ___

å *as in* bat; e *or* eh *as in* bet

English	Pronunciation	Norwegian Spelling
	EXAMPLE	
It is ___	DEH år ___	Det er ___
good	GAWT	godt
It is good	DEH år GAWT	Det er godt
bad	DAWR-lee	dårlig
cheap	BIL-lee	billig
expensive	KAWST-bart	kostbart
large	STORT	stort
small	LEE-teh	litet
clean	RAYNT	rent
dirty	SHITT-ent	skittent
cold	KAHLT	kaldt
warm	VARMT	varmt
much	MAY-get	meget
far	LAHNKT	langt
near	NÅRT	nært
here	HÅR	her
there	DÅR	der

å *as in* bat; e *or* eh *as in* bet

IMPORTANT SIGNS

STOPP	Stop
FARE	Danger
LANGSOMT	Slow
TILBAKE	Detour
VÆR FORSIKTIG	Caution
ENVEG	One Way
INGEN GJENNOMGANG	No Thoroughfare
STIGNING	Grade Crossing
BLINDGATE	Dead End
HOLD TIL HØYRE	Keep to the Right
FARLIG SVING	Dangerous Curve
JERNBANE	Railroad

Brekkestø

BRO	Bridge
KRYSSVEG	Crossroad
STENGT	Keep Out
INGEN ADGANG	No Admittance
PARKERING FORBUDT	No Parking
RØKNING FORBUDT	No Smoking
TOALETT	Lavatory
MENN	Men
KVINNER	Women
ÅPEN	Open
STENGT	Closed
INNGANG	Entrance
UTGANG	Exit

Streets of Bergen

Trondheim

The Viking Museum, Oslo

51

ALPHABETICAL
WORD LIST

A

a, an	ayn *or* et	en et
adhesive tape	PLA-ster	plaster
am		
I am ___	YAY år ___	Jeg er ___
American		
I am an American	YAY år ah- m<u>ay</u>-ree-KA-ner	Jeg er amerikaner
and	o	og
antiseptic	ahn-tee-SEP-tisk- MID-del	antiseptiskmiddel
apples	EP-LER	epler
are		
Are you ___?	ĂR dee ___?	Er De ___?
They are ___	DEE år ___	De er ___
We are ___	VEE år ___	Vi er ___

ă *as in* bat; e *or* eh *as in* bet

English	Pronunciation	Norwegian Spelling
aspirin	ah-spee-REEN	aspirin

B

English	Pronunciation	Norwegian Spelling
bad	DAWR-lee	dårlig
bandage	bahn-DA-sheh	bandasje
barber	bar-B<u>AY</u>R	barber
the barber	bar-B<u>AY</u>-ren	barberen
bath		
I want to take a bath	yay VIL TA et B<u>AH</u>D	Jeg vil ta et bad
beans	BUN-NER	bønner
bed	SENG	seng
beef	BIF	biff
beer	UL	øll
a glass of beer	et glahss UL	et glas øll
blades		
razor blades	bar-B<u>AY</u>R-blahd	barberblad
blankets	ool-TEP-per	ulltepper

English	Pronunciation	Norwegian Spelling
boiled water	KOAKT VAHN	kokt vann
bottle	FLA-skeh	flaske
a bottle of wine	ayn FLA-skeh VEEN	en flaske vin
bread	BR**ER**	brød
bridge	BRO	bro
the bridge	BROAN	broen
Bring help!	skahf YELP!	Skaff hjelp!
brush		
shaving brush	bar-B**AY**R-koast	barberkost
toothbrush	TAHN-bursh-teh	tannbørste
bus	BOOSS	buss
the bus	BOOSS-en	bussen
When does the bus leave?	NAWR gawr BOOSS-en?	Når går bussen?
butter	SM**ER**R	smør
buttons	K‿NAHP-per	knapper
buy		
I want to buy it	yay VIL CH**ER**-peh deh	Jeg vil kjøpe det

å as in bat; e *or* eh *as in* bet

English	Pronunciation	Norwegian Spelling
Where can I buy ___?	VOR kahn yay faw CH<u>ER</u>-peh ___?	Hvor kan jeg få kjøpe ___?

C

English	Pronunciation	Norwegian Spelling
cabbage	KAWL	kål
camp	LAYR	leir
the camp	LAY-ren	leiren
can		
Where can I buy ___?	VOR kahn yay faw CH<u>ER</u>-peh ___?	Hvor kan jeg få kjøpe ___?
Where can I get ___?	VOR kahn yay FAW ___?	Hvor kan jeg få ___?
carrots	GOO-leh-rut-ter	gulerøtter
cheap	BIL-lee	billig
cheese	OAST	ost
chicken	CHIL-LING	kylling
chocolate	sho-ko-LA-deh	sjokolade
church	CHEER-keh	kirke
the church	CHEER-ken	kirken
cigarettes	sig-ah-RET-TER	sigaretter

Inner Harbor, Bergen

English	Pronunciation	Norwegian Spelling
cigars	see-GA-rer	sigarer
city	BEE	by
the city	BEE-en	byen
clean	RAYNT	rent
clothing store	KLAY-fawr-ret-ning	kleforretning
coffee	KA-fay	kaffe
a cup of coffee	ayn kawp KA-fay	en kopp kaffe
cold	KAHLT	kaldt
comb	KAHM	kam

ă *as in* bat; e *or* eh *as in* bet

English	Pronunciation	Norwegian Spelling
come		
Come here!	KAWM HEET!	Kom hit!
Come in!	KAWM in!	Kom inn!
Come quickly!	KAWM STRAHKS!	Kom straks!
cost		
How much does this cost?	vor MAY-get KAW-ster DET-TEH?	Hvor meget koster dette?
cotton	BO-mool	bomull
cover		
Take cover!	SERK DEK-ning!	Søk dekning!
cup	KAWP	kopp
a cup of coffee	ayn kawp KA-fay	en kopp kaffe

D

Danger!	FA-reh!	Fare!
day	DA	dag
Good day	go DA	God dag

English	Pronunciation	Norwegian Spelling
dentist	TAHN-lay-geh	tannlæge
the dentist	TAHN-lay-gen	tannlægen
dirty	SHITT-ent	skittent
disinfectant	dess-in-fee-SAY-ren-deh MID-del	desinfiserende middel
doctor	DAWK-tor	doktor
the doctor	DAWK-to-ren	doktoren
Take me to a doctor	SEN may til ayn DAWK-tor	Send meg til en doktor
Draw me a map	TAYN et KART fawr MAY	Tegn et kart for meg
drinking water	DRIK-keh-VAHN	drikkevann
drugstore *or* pharmacy	ah-po-TAYK	apotek

E

English	Pronunciation	Norwegian Spelling
east	UST	øst
eat		
I want to eat	yay VIL SPEE-seh	Jeg vil spise

ă *as in* bat; e *or* eh *as in* bet

English	Pronunciation	Norwegian Spelling
eggs	EG	egg
eight	AWT-TEH	åtte
eighteen	AHT-TEN	atten
eighty	AWT-tee	åtti
eleven	EL-VEH	elleve
evening	AHF-TEN *or* KVEL	aften kveld
Good evening	go AHF-TEN *or* go KVEL	God aften God kveld
Excuse me	OON-shil	Unnskyld
expensive	KAWST-bart	Kostbart

F

far	LAHNKT	langt
How far is it?	vor LAHNKT år DEH?	Hvor langt er det?
Is it far?	år deh LAHNKT?	Er det langt?
fifteen	FEM-TEN	femten
fifty	FEM-tee	femti

å *as in* bat; e *or* eh *as in* bet   **59**

Nidaros Cathedral, Trondheim

English	Pronunciation	Norwegian Spelling
filling station	ben-SEEN-sta-shoan	bensinstasjon
Fine, thank you	tahk, BRA	Takk, bra
fish	FISK	fisk
five	FEM	fem
food	MAHT	mat
Please give me food	VÄR saw SNIL aw YEE may MAHT	Vær så snild å gi meg mat
fork	GAHF-fel	gaffel
forty	FUR-tee	førti
four	FEE-REH	fire
fourteen	F͜YOR-TEN	fjorten
Friday	FRAY-da	fredag
friend	VEN	venn
I am a friend	YAY år ayn VEN	Jeg er en venn
fruit	FROOKT	frukt

G

garage	ga-RA-sheh	garasje
Gas!	GAHSS!	Gass!

ä *as in* bat; e *or* eh *as in* bet

English	Pronunciation	Norwegian Spelling
gasoline	ben-SEEN	bensin
get		
Where can I get __?	VOR kahn yay FAW __?	Hvor kan jeg få __?
Give me __	YEE may __	Gi meg __
Please give me __	VÅR saw SNIL aw YEE may __	Vær så snild å gi meg __
Glad to know you	HIG-gel-ee aw SA̱Y dem	Hyggelig å se Dem
glass	GLAHSS	glass
a glass of beer	et GLAHSS UL	et glass øll
go		
Go quickly!	GAW STRAHKS!	Gå straks!
Please go with me	VÅR saw SNIL aw GAW meh MAY	Vær så snild å gå med meg
good	GAWT	godt
Good day	go DA	God dag
Good evening	go AHF-TEN *or* go KVEL	God aften God kveld

ă *as in* bat; e *or* eh *as in* bet

English	Pronunciation	Norwegian Spelling
Good luck!	LIK-keh TIL!	Lykke til!
Good morning	go MAWRN	God morgen
Good-by	ahd-Y<u>ER</u>	adjø
grapes	DROO-er	druer
grocery	ko-lo-nee-AHL-hahnd-el	kolonialhandel

H

half	HAHL	halv
half past four	HAHL FEM	halv fem
ham	SHIN-keh	skinke
handkerchief	TURK-leh	tørkle
have		
Have a seat!	TA plahss!	Ta plass!
Let me have ___	LA may FAW ___	La meg få ___
Have you ___?	HAR dee ___?	Har De ___?
I don't have ___	YAY har IK-keh ___	Jeg har ikke ___

ă *as in* bat; e *or* eh *as in* bet   **63**

English	Pronunciation	Norwegian Spelling
I have ___	YAY har ___	Jeg har ___
We don't have ___	VEE har IK-keh ___	Vi har ikke ___
We have ___	VEE har ___	Vi har ___
he	HAHN	han
He is ___	HAHN ăr ___	Han er ___
Hello	ha-LO	Hallo
Help!	YELP!	Hjelp!
Bring help!	skahf YELP!	Skaff hjelp!
Please help me	VĂR saw SNIL aw YELP-eh MAY	Vær så snild å hjelpe meg
here	HĂR	her
Come here!	KAWM HEET!	Kom hit!
highway	HO-ved-VAY	hovedveg
the highway	HO-ved-VAY-en	hovedvegen
hospital	ho-spee-TAHL	hospital
the hospital	ho-spee-TA-leh	hospitalet
Take me to the hospital	SEN may til ho-spee-TA-leh	Send meg til hospitalet
hot water	VARMT VAHN	varmt vann

ă *as in* bat; e *or* eh *as in* bet

English	Pronunciation	Norwegian Spelling
hotel	ho-TEL	hotel
the hotel	ho-TEL-eh	hotellet
Where is the hotel?	VOR är ho-TEL-eh?	Hvor er hotellet?
house	HOOSS	hus
how		
How are you?	VOR-dahn HAR dee deh?	Hvordan har De det?
How do you say ___?	va HAY-TER ___?	Hvad heter ___?
How far is ___?	vor LAHNKT är deh til ___?	Hvor langt er det til ___?
How far is it?	vor LAHNKT är DEH?	Hvor langt er det?
How much does this cost?	vor MAY-get KAW-ster DET-TEH?	Hvor meget koster dette?
hundred	HOON-DREH	hundre
hungry		
I am hungry	YAY är SOOL-ten	Jeg er sulten
We are hungry	VEE är SOOLT-neh	Vi er sultne

ä *as in* bat; e *or* eh *as in* bet

I

I	YAY	jeg
I am ___	YAY är ___	Jeg er ___
I don't have ___	YAY har IK-keh ___	Jeg har ikke ___
I have ___	YAY har ___	Jeg har ___
I want to ___	yay VIL ___	Jeg vil ___
in Norwegian	paw NAWRSHK	på norsk
ink	BLEK	blekk
iodine	YAWD	jodd
is	ÄR	er
He is ___	HAHN är ___	Han er ___
Is it ___?	ÄR deh ___?	Er det ___?
It is ___	DEH är ___	Det er ___
It is not ___	DEH är IK-keh ___	Det er ikke ___
it	DEH	det

K

kilometer	chee-lo-MET-er	kilometer
knife	K‿NEEV	kniv

ă *as in* bat: e *or* eh *as in* bet

English	Pronunciation	Norwegian Spelling
know		
I don't know	yay VAYT ik-keh	Jeg vet ikke

L

English	Pronunciation	Norwegian Spelling
lamb	FAW-reh-CHUT	fårekjøtt
large	STORT	stort
laundry	va-skay-REE	vaskeri
laxative	AHV-fer-ringss-MID-del	avføringsmiddel
leave		
When does the bus leave?	NAWR gawr BOOSS-en?	Når går bussen?
When does the train leave?	NAWR gawr TAWG-eh?	Når går toget?
left	VEN-streh	venstre
to the left	til VEN-streh	til venstre
let		
Let me have __	LA may FAW __	La meg få __

English	Pronunciation	Norwegian Spelling
lost		
I am lost	YAY har GAWT may BORT	Jeg har gått meg bort
luck		
Good luck!	LIK-keh TIL!	Lykke til!

M

main street	HO-ved-GA-teh	hovedgate
the main street	HO-ved-GA-ten	hovedgaten
map	KART	kart
Draw me a map	TAYN et KART fawr MAY	Tegn et kart for meg
market	TAWRV	torv
the market	TAWR-veh	torvet
matches	FEER-shtik-ker	fyrstikker
mattress	ma-DRAHSS	madrass
may		
May I___?	kahn yay FAW ___?	Kan jeg få ___?

å *as in* bat; e *or* eh *as in* bet

English	Pronunciation	Norwegian Spelling
maybe	KAHN-sheh	*kanskje
meat	CHUT	kjøtt
mechanic	may-KA-nee-ker	mekaniker
milk	MELK	melk
minute		
Wait a minute!	VENT lit!	Vent litt!
Miss	FRER-ken	Frøken
Monday	MAHN-da	mandag
morning	MAWRN	morgen
Good morning	go MAWRN	God morgen

Hopperstand Stave Church

English	Pronunciation	Norwegian Spelling
movie	CHEE-no	kino
the movie	CHEE-noan	kinoen
When does the movie start?	NAWR B'YIN-ner CHEE-noan?	Når begynner kinoen?
Mr.	HÄR	Herr
Mrs.	FROO	Fru
much	MAY-get	meget

N

name		
My name is ___	yay HAY-TER ___	Jeg heter ___
What is your name?	va HAY-TER DEE?	Hvad heter Dee?
near	NÄRT	nært
Is it near by?	är deh ee när-HAY-ten?	Er det i nærheten?
the nearest town	den NÄR-mest-eh BEE	den nærmeste by
needle	NAWL	nål
nine	NEE	ni

ä *as in* bat; e *or* eh *as in* bet

English	Pronunciation	Norwegian Spelling
nineteen	NIT-TEN	nitten
ninety	NIT-tee	nitti
No	NAY	Nei
north		
Which way is north?	VOR är NOR?	Hvor er nord?
Norwegian	NAWRSHK	norsk
in Norwegian	paw NAWRSHK	på norsk
not	IK-keh	ikke

O

o'clock		
It is one o'clock	KLAWK-ken är ET	Klokken er ett
It is two o'clock	KLAWK-ken är TO	Klokken er to
one o'clock	ET	ett
two o'clock	TO	to
one	AYN	en
onions	LERK	løk

ä *as in* bat; e *or* eh *as in* bet

paper	pa-PEER	papir
past		
half past four	HAHL FEM	halv fem
pay		
I'll pay you	yay VIL B'TA-leh dem	Jeg vil betale Dem
I want to pay	yay VIL B'TA-leh	Jeg vil betale
pears	PĂR-er	pærer
peas	ĂR-ter	erter
pen	PEN	penn
pencil	bl<u>ee</u>-AHNT	blyant
pepper	PEP-PER	pepper
pillow	POO-teh	pute
pin	NAWL	nål
safety pins	sik-ker-h<u>a</u>yts-NAW-ler	sikkerhetsnåler
pipe	PEE-peh	pipe
plate	tah<u>l</u>-LĂR-ken	tallerken

ă *as in* b*a*t; e *or* eh *as in* b*e*t

Stortinget (Parliament), Oslo

English	Pronunciation	Norwegian Spelling
Please	VǍR saw SNIL aw ___	Vær så snild å ___
Please help me	VǍR saw SNIL aw YELP-eh MAY	Vær så snild å hjelpe meg
policeman	po-lee-TEE	politi
the policeman	po-lee-TEE-eh	politiet
police station	po-lee-TEE-sta-shoan	politistasjon
the police station	po-lee-TEE-sta-sho-nen	politistasjonen
polish		
shoe polish	sko-SVǍR-teh	skosverte
pork	FLESK	flesk
porter	BǍR-er	bærer
post office	PAWST-koan-tor	postkontor
the post office	PAWST-koan-to-reh	postkontoret
potatoes	po-TAY-ter	poteter

Q

Quickly!	STRAHKS!	Straks!

ǎ *as in* bat; e *or* eh *as in* bet

English	Pronunciation	Norwegian Spelling
Come quickly!	KAWM STRAHKS!	Kom straks!
Go quickly!	GAW STRAHKS!	Gå straks!

R

railroad	yărn-BA-neh	jernbane
the railroad	yărn-BA-nen	jernbanen
railroad station	sta-SHOAN	stasjon
the railroad station	sta-SHO-nen	stasjonen
Where is the railroad station?	VOR ăr sta-SHO-nen?	Hvor er stasjonen?
raincoat	RAYN-frahk	regnfrakk
razor	bar-BAYP-her-vel	barberhøvel
razor blades	bar-BAYR-blahd	barberblad
repeat		
Please repeat	VĂR saw SNIL aw YEN-TA	Vær så snild å gjenta
rest		
I want to rest	yay VIL VEE-leh	Jeg vil hvile

ă *as in* băt; e *or* eh *as in* bet   **75**

Ringve Museum, Trondheim

English	Pronunciation	Norwegian Spelling
restaurant	ka-F<u>AY</u>	kafé
the restaurant	ka-F<u>AY</u>-en	kaféen
Where is the restaurant?	VOR år ka-F<u>AY</u>-en?	Hvor er kaféen?
right	HAY-reh	høire
to the right	til HAY-reh	til høire
river	ELV	elv
the river	ELV-ah	elva

å *as in* bat; e *or* eh *as in* bet

English	Pronunciation	Norwegian Spelling
road	VAY	veg
the road	VAY-en	vegen
Which is the road to Oslo?	VOR gawr VAY-en til O-slo?	Hvor går vegen til Oslo?
room	ROOM	rom

S

English	Pronunciation	Norwegian Spelling
safety pins	sik-ker-hayts-NAW-ler	sikkerhetsnåler
sailors	SHER-FOL-keh-neh	sjøfolkene
salad	sa-LAHT	salat
salt	SAHLT	salt
Saturday	LUR-da	lørdag
say		
How do you say ___?	va HAY-TER ___?	Hvad heter ___?

ă *as in* bat; e *or* eh *as in* bet

English	Pronunciation	Norwegian Spelling
seat		
Have a seat!	TA plahss!	Ta plass!
servant	T‿YAY-ner	tjener
seven	SHOO	sju
seventeen	SUT-TEN	sytten
seventy	SUT-tee	sytti
shave		
shaving brush	bar-BAYR-koast	barberkost
shaving soap	bar-BAYR-saw-peh	barbersåpe
she	HOON	hun
sheets	LA-ken-er	lakener
shirt	SHOR-teh	skjorte
shoemaker	sko-MA-ker	skomaker
the shoemaker	sko-MA-ker-en	skomakeren
shoes	SKO	sko
shoe laces	sko-LISS-ser	skolisser
shoe polish	sko-SVÅR-teh	skosverte

English	Pronunciation	Norwegian Spelling
show		
Will you show me the way?	KAHN dee VEE-seh may VAY-en?	Kan De vise meg vegen?
sick		
I am sick	YAY är SEEK	Jeg er syk
We are sick	VEE är SEE-keh	Vi er syke
six	SEKS	seks
sixteen	SAYSS-TEN	seksten
sixty	SEKS-tee	seksti

The Lysoen Island

English	Pronunciation	Norwegian Spelling
sleep		
I want to sleep	yay VIL SAW-veh	Jeg vil sove
slowly	lahng-SAWMT	langsomt
Speak slowly	SNAHK lahng-SAWMT	Snakk langsomt
small	LEE-teh	litet
soap	SAW-peh	såpe
shaving soap	bar-BAYR-saw-peh	barbersåpe
soup	SOOP-PEH	suppe
south	SEED	syd
speak		
Speak slowly	SNAHK lahng-SAWMT	Snakk langsomt
spoon	SHAY	skje
spring	CHIL-deh	kilde
start		
When does the movie start?	NAWR B'YIN-ner CHEE-noan?	Når begynner kinoen?

English	Pronunciation	Norwegian Spelling
station	sta-SHOAN	stasjon
the station	sta-SHO-nen	stasjonen
Stop!	STAHN-seh! or STAWP!	Stanse! Stopp!
straight ahead	ret FRAHM	rett fram
street		
main street	HO-ved-GA-teh	hovedgate
streetcar	TRIK	trikk
the streetcar	TRIK-ken	trikken
Where is the streetcar?	VOR är TRIK-ken?	Hvor er trikken?
sugar	SOOK-ker	sukker
Sunday	SUN-da	søndag

T

English	Pronunciation	Norwegian Spelling
tailor	SKRED-der	skredder
the tailor	SKRED-der-en	skredderen
take		
I want to take a bath	yay VIL TA et BAHD	Jeg vil ta et bad

ă *as in* bat; e *or* eh *as in* bet   **81**

English	Pronunciation	Norwegian Spelling
Take cover!	S<u>E</u>RK DEK-ning!	Søk dekning!
Take me to a doctor	SEN may til ayn DAWK-tor	Send meg til en doktor
Take me to the hospital	SEN may til ho-spee-TA-leh	Send meg til hospitalet
tea	T<u>AY</u>	te
telegraph office	tel-eg-RAHF-koan-tor	telegrafkontor
the telegraph office	tel-eg-RAHF-koan-to-reh	telegrafkontoret
telephone	tel-eh-FOAN	telefon
the telephone	tel-eh-FO-nen	telefonen
ten	TEE	ti
Thank you	TAHK	Takk
there	DĂR	der
they	DEE	De
They are ___	DEE ǎr ___	De er ___

82

ǎ *as in* bǎt; e *or* eh *as in* bet

English	Pronunciation	Norwegian Spelling
think		
I think so	yay TROR deh	Jeg tror det
I don't think so	yay TROR IK-keh DEH	Jeg tror ikke det
thirsty		
I am thirsty	YAY år TURSHT	Jeg er tørst
We are thirsty	VEE år TURSH-teh	Vi er tørste
thirteen	TRET-TEN	tretten
thirty	TRED-VEH	tredve
this	DET-teh	dette
This is ___	DET-teh år ___	Dette er ___
What is this?	VA år DET-TEH?	Hvad er dette?
thousand	TOO-sen	tusen
thread	TRAW	tråd
three	TRAY	tre
Thursday	TAWRSH-da	torsdag

English	Pronunciation	Norwegian Spelling
time		
What time is it?	va ăr KLAWK-KEN?	Hvad er klokken?
tired		
I am tired	YAY ăr TRET	Jeg er trett
We are tired	VEE ăr TRET-teh	Vi er trette
to	TIL	til
to a doctor	til ayn DAWK-tor	til en doktor
to the hospital	til ho-spee-TA-leh	til hospitalet
to the left	til VEN-streh	til venstre
to the right	til HAY-reh	til høire
tobacco	to-BAHK	tobakk
today	ee-DA	idag
toilet	twa-LET	toalett
the toilet	twa-LET-teh	toalettet
Where is the toilet?	VOR ăr twa-LET-teh?	Hvor er toalettet?
tomorrow	ee-MAWRN	imorgen

ă *as in* bat; e *or* eh *as in* bet

English	Pronunciation	Norwegian Spelling
too	FAWR	for
It is too ___	DEH år fawr ___	Det er for ___
toothbrush	TAHN-bursh-teh	tannbørste
tooth paste	TAHN-kraym	tannkrem
towel	HAWN-kleh	håndkle
town		
the large town	BEE-en	byen
the small town	LAHNTS-bee-en	landsbyen
Where is the nearest town?	VOR år den NÅR-mest-eh BEE?	Hvor er den nærmeste by?
train	TAWG	tog
the train	TAWG-eh	toget
When does the train leave?	NAWR gawr TAWG-eh?	Når går toget?
Tuesday	TEERSH-da	tirsdag
twelve	TAWL	tolv
twenty	TEE-VEH	tyve
twenty-one	AYN o TEE-VEH	en og tyve

ă *as in* bat; e *or* eh *as in* bet

English	Pronunciation	Norwegian Spelling
twenty-two	TO o TEE-VEH	to og tyve
two	TO	to

U

understand		
Do you under-stand?	fawr-STAWR dee?	Forstår De?
I don't under-stand	YAY fawr-STAWR IK-keh	Jeg forstår ikke
underwear	oon-er-TAY	undertøy

V

veal	KAHL-veh-CHUT	kalvekjøtt
vegetables	GRUN-SA-ker	grønnsaker
very	MAY-get	meget
It is very __	DEH år MAY-get __	Det er meget __

W

Wait a minute!	VENT lit!	Vent litt!

ă *as in* bat; e *or* eh *as in* bet

English	Pronunciation	Norwegian Spelling
want		
I want to __	yay VIL __	Jeg vil __
warm	VARMT	varmt
wash up		
I want to wash up	yay VIL VA-skeh may	Jeg vil vaske meg
Watch out!	PAHSS paw!	Pass på!
water	VAHN	vann
boiled water	KOAKT VAHN	kokt vann
drinking water	DRIK-keh-VAHN	drikkevann
hot water	VARMT VAHN	varmt vann
way		
Which way is north?	VOR år NOR?	Hvor er nord?
Will you show me the way?	KAHN dee VEE-seh may VAY-en?	Kan De vise meg vegen?
we	VEE	vi
We are __	VEE år __	Vi er __

ă *as in* bat; e *or* eh *as in* bet

Vigeland Park, Oslo

English	Pronunciation	Norwegian Spelling
We don't have ___	VEE har IK-keh ___	Vi har ikke ___
We have ___	VEE har ___	Vi har ___
Wednesday	OANSS-da	onsdag
well (*for water*)	BRUN	bronn
west	VEST	vest
what	VA	hvad
What is this?	VA är DET-TEH?	Hvad er dette?
What time is it?	va är KLAWK-KEN?	Hvad er klokken?
when	NAWR	når
When does the bus leave?	NAWR gawr BOOSS-en?	Når går bussen?
When does the train leave?	NAWR gawr TAWG-eh?	Når går toget?
When does the movie start?	NAWR B'YIN-ner CHEE-noan?	Når begynner kinoen?
where	VOR	hvor
Where can I buy ___?	VOR kahn yay faw CHER-peh ___?	Hvor kan jeg få kjøpe ___?

ä *as in* bat; e *or* eh *as in* bet   **89**

English	Pronunciation	Norwegian Spelling
Where can I get ___?	VOR kahn yay FAW ___?	Hvor kan jeg få ___?
Where is ___?	VOR år ___?	Hvor er ___?
Where is there ___?	VOR år deh ___?	Hvor er det ___?

which

Which is the road to Oslo?	VOR gawr VAY-en til O-slo?	Hvor går vegen til Oslo?
Which way is north?	VOR år NOR?	Hvor er nord?

who — VEM — hvem

Who is ___?	VEM år ___?	Hvem er ___?

wine — VEEN — vin

a bottle of wine	ayn FLA-skeh VEEN	en flaske vin

wounded — SAW-ret — såret

I am wounded	YAY år SAW-ret	Jeg er såret
We are wounded	VEE år SAW-ret	Vi er såret

ä *as in* bat; e *or* eh *as in* bet

Swords in the Rock, Hafrsfjord

Y

Yes	YA	Ja
yesterday	ee-GAWR	igår
you	DEE	De
Are you ___?	ÄR dee ___?	Er De ___?
Have you ___?	HAR dee ___?	Har De ___?

91

Glaciers at Nigardsbreen